ONCE UPON A TIME II

THE KING WITHOUT A THRONE

JILLIAN LIN
Illustrations by SHI MENG

Confucius (Kong Fuzi) (551–479 BC),
teacher and philosopher, Zhou Dynasty

Once upon a time in China…

… lived a wise man called Confucius. He was so wise that even today, people still study the ideas he came up with more than 2,000 years ago.

Before Confucius was born, his mother kept on praying for a baby boy as she already had nine girls. One night, she had a dream. Five figures were coming towards her, followed by a creature with a horn on its head, like a unicorn.

At the time, people believed that whenever this creature was spotted, a special person would be born or would be close to dying.

'My lady,' one of the figures said in the dream, 'you will have a son who is special. He will be a king. However, he will become a king without a throne.'

In her dream, Confucius' mother found herself tying a ribbon around the unicorn's horn. Then she woke up.

True enough, a baby boy was born, which made both his parents happy. But when Confucius was only three years old, his father died. His family became very poor, and his mother struggled to feed all the children.

Confucius missed his father very much. That was why his mother taught him to remember his father by putting food on special bowls and praying to him every day.

While the other children were playing, Confucius would spend hours and hours carefully laying out his bowls and plates.

At the time, there were no schools and hardly any books, so children would learn things from listening to

songs and poems. As Confucius loved learning, he memorized everything his mother taught him and asked everyone to teach him all they knew. People soon found out that he was very clever and knew a lot. Confucius started teaching to earn money. He was such a good teacher that more and more students wanted to learn from him. Confucius spent the whole day studying and teaching, telling stories of old kings and the great things they had done.

His students wrote all he taught onto bamboo strips, which were then made into books.

Confucius said, 'We should respect our parents, our grandparents, and all those who came before us. What we have today, we owe to them. For example, someone discovered fire a long time ago. People then used fire to cook, make pots, and bend metal so they could make better tools. They used these tools to build houses. Could you imagine what life would be like without that first person who discovered fire?'

When Confucius was about 50 years old, he found a job in the government. Now he could finally try out his ideas and teachings in real life.

He told people to know their place and follow the rules. Children had to listen to their parents. Parents had to be good to their children and not tell them any lies.

Everyone had to listen to the king, but the king should also treat the people well.

Confucius said, 'Always do the right thing. Treat others as you would like others to treat you.'

Soon, it was safer in the streets, people were happier, and life was better for everyone.

At the time, China was not one big country as it is today, but it was split into kingdoms. Confucius' kingdom was doing very well. But the king of another kingdom got jealous and came up with a mean plan. He sent beautiful horses and dancing girls to Confucius' king, hoping that he would enjoy these instead of ruling the kingdom.

Sadly, Confucius' king did exactly as the mean king had hoped – he spent three whole days riding the horses and enjoying the performances. Confucius was so angry with his king that he decided to leave the kingdom. A group of students followed him.

Confucius and his students traveled from kingdom to kingdom for many years, giving advice to kings about ruling their kingdoms.

Sometimes the kings listened to his wise words, but they never asked him to work for them. Without any work,

Confucius and his followers had very little to eat and often had to sleep in the open air.

One day, Confucius met some hunters who had found a strange-looking creature. When Confucius saw the creature, he burst out crying.

It was a unicorn with a frayed piece of ribbon tied to its horn.

'My time has come,' he sobbed.

Confucius wasn't sad that he was close to the end of his life. Instead, he was disappointed with himself.

He thought he had failed to make China a better place with his ideas.

How wrong he was.

Not long after his death, kings and emperors started using his ideas to rule their people. Special temples were built all over Asia to honor him.

Today, Confucius is known as one of the greatest teachers in the history of China.

In the end, his mother's dream had come true. Confucius had become as wise and important as a king, but he had become a king without a throne.

DID YOU KNOW?

1 ~ At birth, Confucius was given the name 'Kong Qiu', Kong being his family name. In China they call him 'Kongzi' or 'Kong Fuzi', which means 'Master Kong'. A priest who visited China from the West gave him the name 'Confucius'.

2 ~ Confucius got married when he was nineteen. He had one daughter and one son, who died five years before his own death. This made him very sad as he had hoped his son would continue teaching his ideas.

3 ~ Before Confucius' time, you could only study and teach if you were rich. Confucius was the first Chinese to make a living out of teaching and he was the first to open a public school to teach ordinary people. He believed that all men – both rich and poor – should have the chance to study and better themselves.

4 ~ Confucius never planned to be a teacher. What he had always wanted was to bring peace to the world. He believed he could stop the wars that were raging at the time if only the kings would listen to his ideas. Sadly, they were more interested in fighting one another than making peace.

5 ~ In Confucius' time, only boys from rich and powerful families were allowed to go to school, where they learned the 'Six Arts': writing, playing music, driving a chariot (a type of carriage), shooting with bow and arrow, carrying out ceremonies, and working with numbers. Girls couldn't go to school. They had to look after the men in their families.

6 ~ Confucius is said to have had around 3,000 students. He taught them history, literature, and philosophy (ideas about people's life and behavior). Instead of standing in front of a class, Confucius let his students talk to one another. That way, they could learn to ask the right questions and think for themselves.

7 ~ Confucius never wrote any books. After his death, his students put his sayings together into a book called *The Analects*. In the next 2,000 years, all students in China had to read this book. Even today, people still study this book to learn about his ideas.

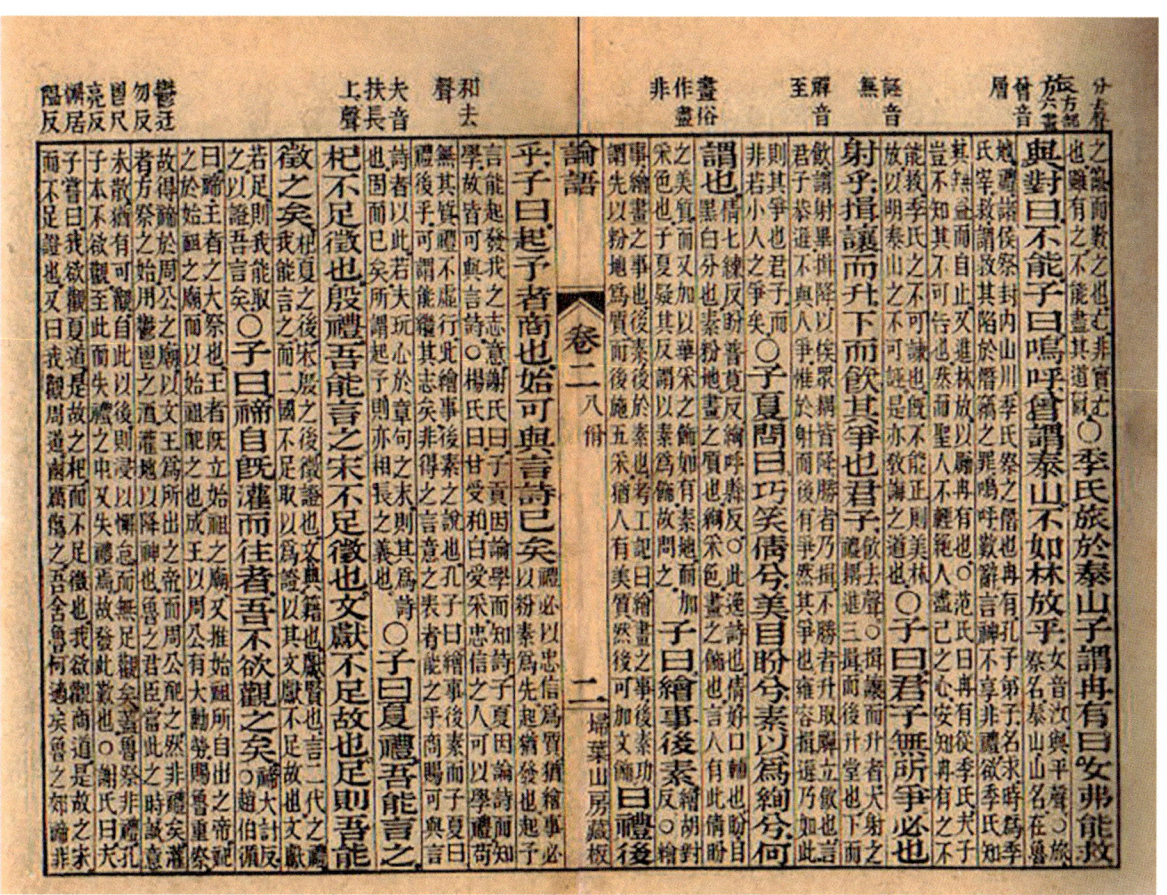

8 ~ Until about 100 years ago, you had to take special exams to get a good job in China. To prepare for these exams, students had to learn Confucius' ideas and sayings by heart. Some of these exams took as long as three days and two nights.

9 ~ Even though Confucius was not a religious leader, the Chinese think as highly of him as Jesus in Western countries or Muhammad in the Muslim world. That is why they honor Confucius with statues, temples, and festivals. On 28 September every year, people remember him by celebrating his birthday. The ceremony includes dancing, food offerings, live music, and prayers.

10 ~ Hundreds of Confucius temples are scattered all over Asia. Most of them are in China, but you can also find temples in Taiwan, Korea, Japan, Malaysia, Vietnam, and Indonesia. The oldest and largest is in Confucius' hometown of Qufu in China's Shandong Province.

TEST YOUR KNOWLEDGE!

1   **What did Confucius do to remember his father?**

a)   He sang the songs that his father taught him.

b)   He drew pictures of him.

c)   He put food on special bowls and prayed to him every day.

2   **How did children learn things in Confucius' time?**

a)   They went to school.

b)   They listened to songs and poems.

c)   They read books.

3   **What did Confucius do to earn money?**

a)   He started teaching.

b)   He built houses using metal tools.

c)   He supplied horses to the king.

4   Why was Confucius angry with the king?

a)   Because the king spent more time riding horses and watching girls dance than ruling his kingdom.

b)   Because the king had said mean things to Confucius.

c)   Because the king didn't treat the people of his kingdom well.

5   Why did Confucius and his students have to sleep in the open air?

a)   Because Confucius was sick and needed to be in the open air to get better.

b)   Because they didn't have any paid work and no money.

c)   Because they enjoyed being in the outdoors.

Answers to the Quiz: 1. c / 2. b / 3. a / 4. a / 5. b

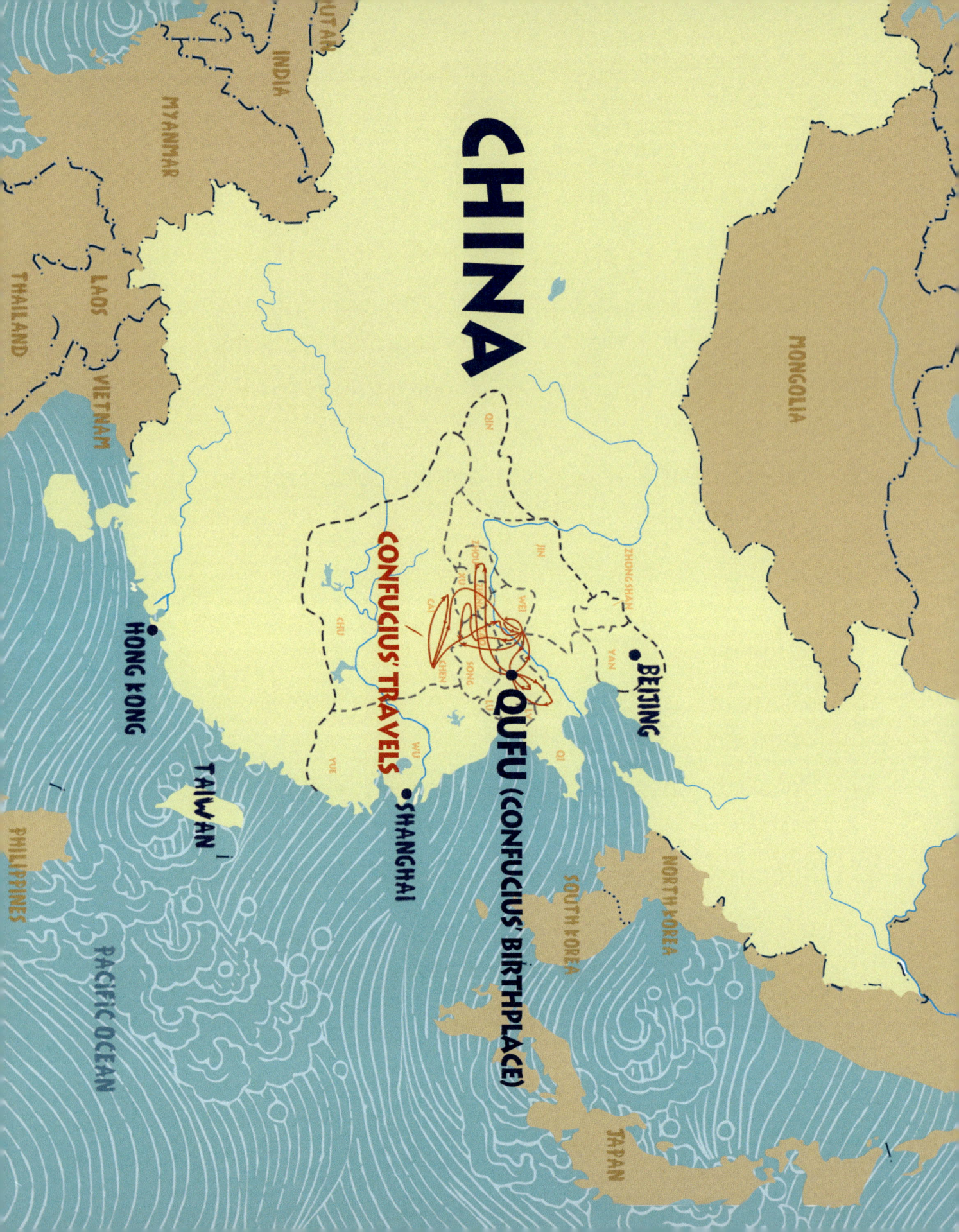

The *Once Upon A Time In China...* Series

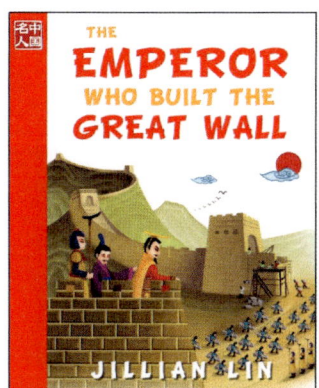
Qin Shihuang

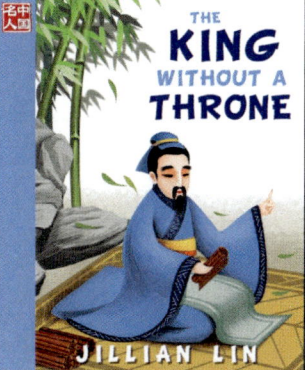
Confucius

Zhu Zaiyu

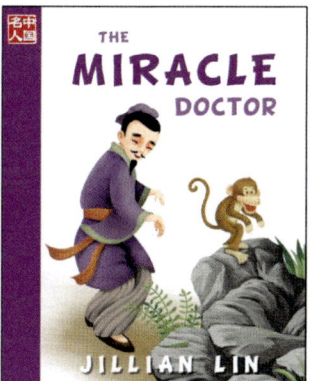
Hua Tuo

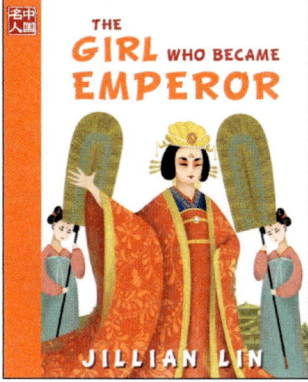
Wu Zetian

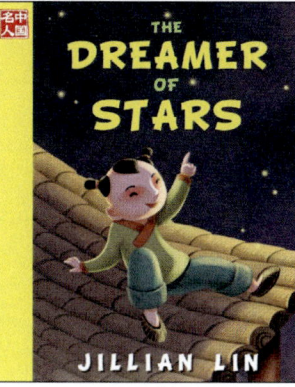
Zhang Heng

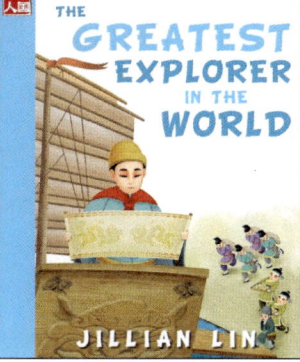
Zheng He

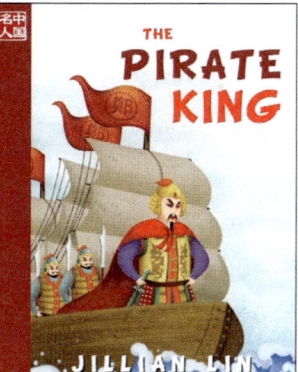
Koxinga

Also available as e-books. For more information, visit

www.jillianlin.com

The King Without A Throne

Copyright © Jillian Lin 2016
Illustrations © Shi Meng 2016

Photos from Wikimedia Commons

All rights reserved. No part of this publication may be copied or reproduced in any format, by any means, electronic or otherwise, without prior consent from the copyright owner and publisher of this book.

Made in the USA
Coppell, TX
26 January 2020